PARTY PLACE MATS

Set the table in style with these place mats!

2

5

8

11

14

LEISURE ARTS, INC. • Maumelle, Arkansas

CELEBRATION

YOUNG AND OLD ALIKE will love having this charming place mat at their birthday party! Bright balloons and streamers paired with scrumptious cupcakes make this a must-have for your next party.

COLOR KEY

▲	Lavender
★	Light Blue
+	Light Brown
✕	Light Pink
•	Lime Green
›	Medium Brown
♥	Red
✳	Rose
◖	Rust
○	Yellow
·	White

<u>Backstitch Floss (4 strands)</u>

——— Black

<u>Straight Stitch Floss (4 strands)</u>

——— Black

Overcast the edges using Lime Green yarn.

CELEBRATION (PART A)
91 × 71 threads

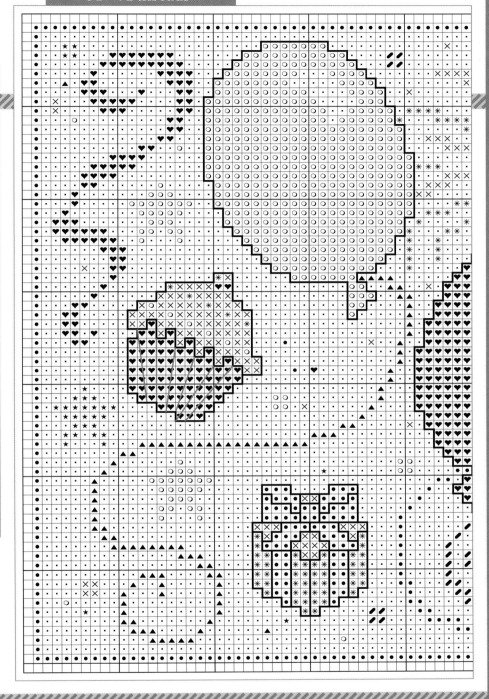

CHART LAYOUT

A	B

CELEBRATION (PART B)
91 × 71 threads

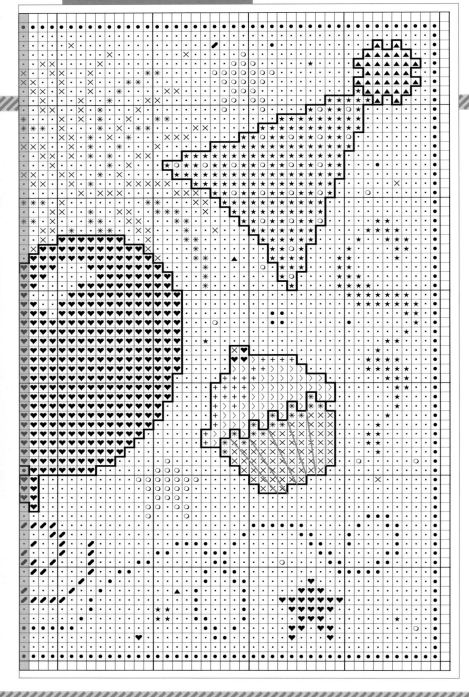

Gray area indicates last row of previous section of design.

Note: Please read all instructions on page 17 before beginning.

COLOR KEY

▲	Lavender
★	Light Blue
+	Light Brown
✕	Light Pink
●	Lime Green
>	Medium Brown
♥	Red
✳	Rose
✦	Rust
○	Yellow
·	White

Backstitch Floss (4 strands)

——— Black

Straight Stitch Floss (4 strands)

——— Black

Overcast the edges using Lime Green yarn.

WINE AND GRAPES

PAIR THIS PLACE MAT with a glass of chardonnay at your next wine-tasting party!

Note: Please read all instructions on page 17 before beginning.

COLOR KEY

−	Cream
✳	Dark Green
◆	Dark Purple
✕	Dark Red
◣	Ecru
✿	Gold
○	Lavender
◥	Light Blue
◇	Light Green
●	Light Yellow
◤	Medium Brown
△	Sage
·	White
♡	Yellow
✛	Yellow Green

<u>Backstitch Floss (4 strands)</u>

———	Dark Green

Overcast the edges using Cream yarn.

CHART LAYOUT

A	B

WINE AND GRAPES (PART A)
91 × 71 threads

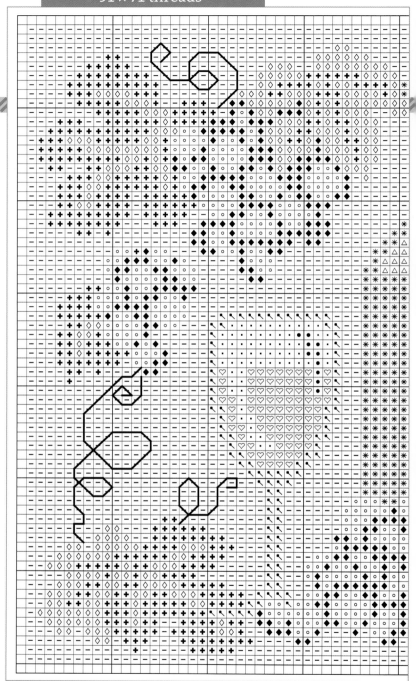

WINE AND GRAPES (PART B)
91 × 71 threads

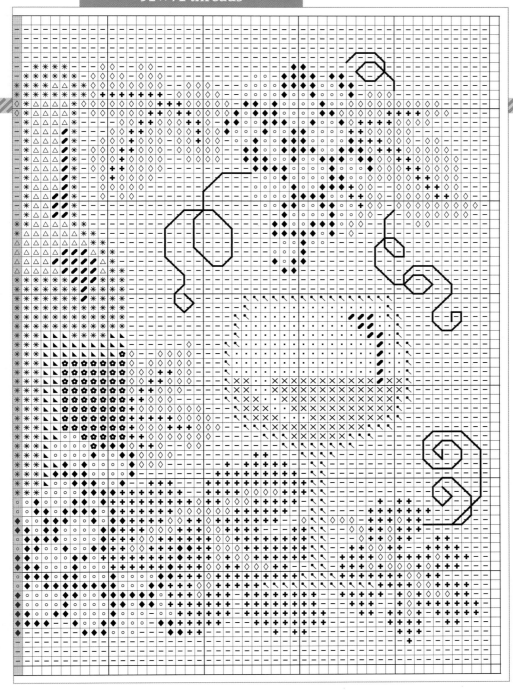

◻ Gray area indicates last row
   of previous section of design.

TRICK OR TREAT

THIS SPOOK-TACULAR DESIGN will look great at your Halloween gathering! Whether using it at a bewitching dinner or as an accent on a table of treats, guests will be enchanted by this design.

Note: Please read all instructions on page 17 before beginning.

COLOR KEY

✳	Black
·	Dark Blue
◆	Lime Green
/	Orange
★	Yellow

Backstitch Floss (4 strands)

┼┼┼┼┼	Black
·····•	Dark Yellow
───	Lime Green
────	Orange
─ ─ ─	Yellow

Overcast the edges using Black yarn.

CHART LAYOUT

A	B

TRICK OR TREAT (PART A)
90 × 70 threads

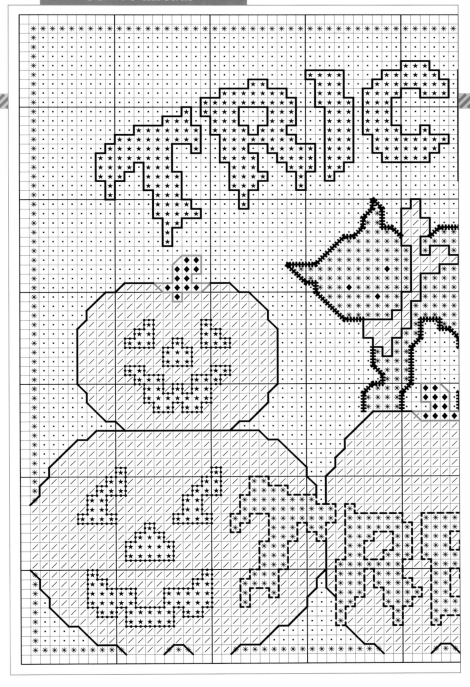

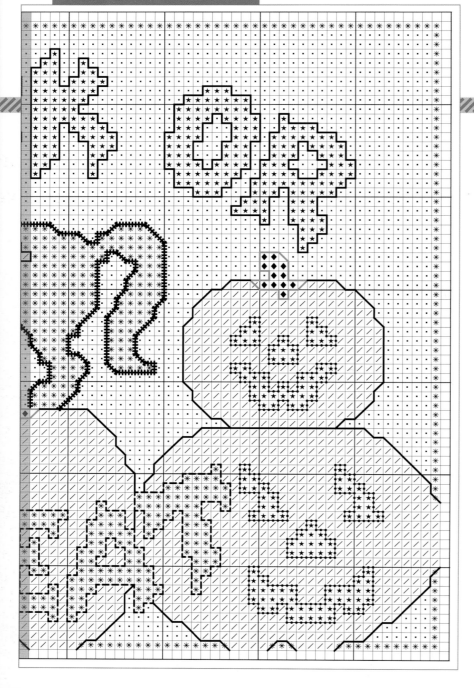

■ Gray area indicates last row of previous section of design.

Note: Please read all instructions on page 17 before beginning.

COLOR KEY

✳	Black
·	Dark Blue
◆	Lime Green
/	Orange
★	Yellow

Backstitch Floss (4 strands)

┼┼┼┼┼	Black
·─·─·	Dark Yellow
───	Lime Green
───	Orange
─ ─ ─	Yellow

Overcast the edges using Black yarn.

POINSETTIA

THIS PRETTY HOLIDAY FLOWER makes an elegant addition to your Christmas dinner table.

Note: Please read all instructions on page 17 before beginning.

COLOR KEY

↟	Dark Green
+	Dark Red
△	Gold
✳	Green
✖	Light Pink
–	Lime Green
♡	Red
╱	Rose
·	White
★	Yellow

Backstitch Floss (4 strands)

——	Black

Overcast the edges using yarn that matches the adjacent stitches.

CHART LAYOUT

A	B

POINSETTIA (PART A)
91 × 71 threads

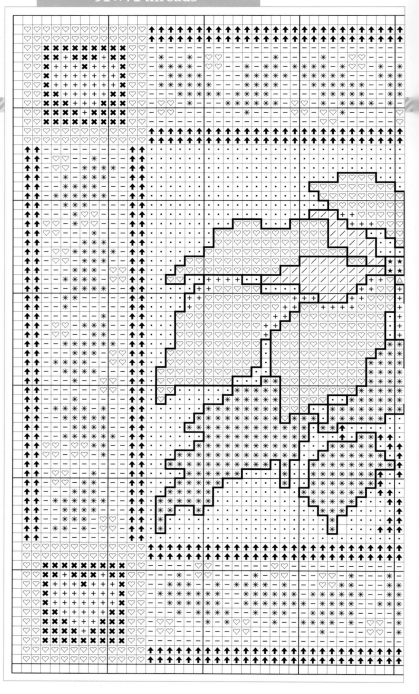

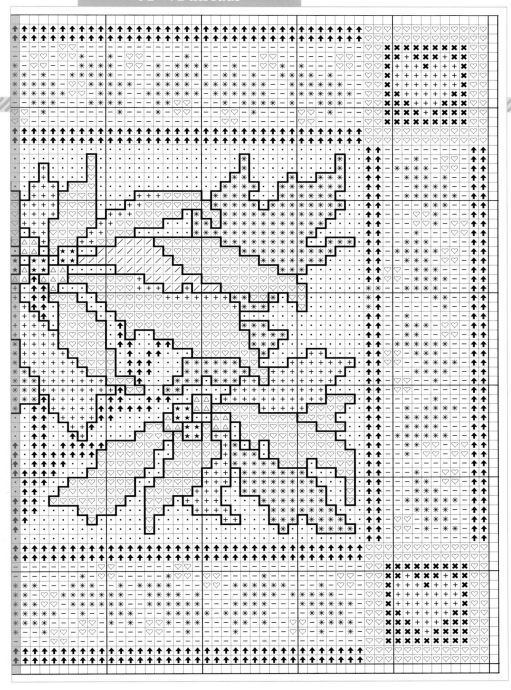

☐ Gray area indicates last row
of previous section of design.

SNOWMAN

INVITE FRIENDS OVER for a winter feast, complete with cookies, cocoa, and this place mat featuring an adorable frosty friend.

COLOR KEY

○	Black
↑	Dark Red
×	Green
·	Light Blue
△	Light Brown
♡	Light Pink
✳	Lime Green
●	Red
+	Rose
★	Rust
❚	Tan
/	White

Backstitch Floss (4 strands)

———	Black
〰〰〰	Dark Blue
– – –	Dark Red
+++++	Green
·—·—·	Light Blue
· · · · · ·	Rose
———	White

Overcast the edges using Red yarn.

CHART LAYOUT

A	B

Notes: Design requires larger than standard piece of canvas. To fit on a standard piece, cut canvas 90 x 70 threads and omit one outer row of Red border stitches on all sides. Please read all instructions on page 17 before beginning.

SNOWMAN (PART A)
92 × 72 threads

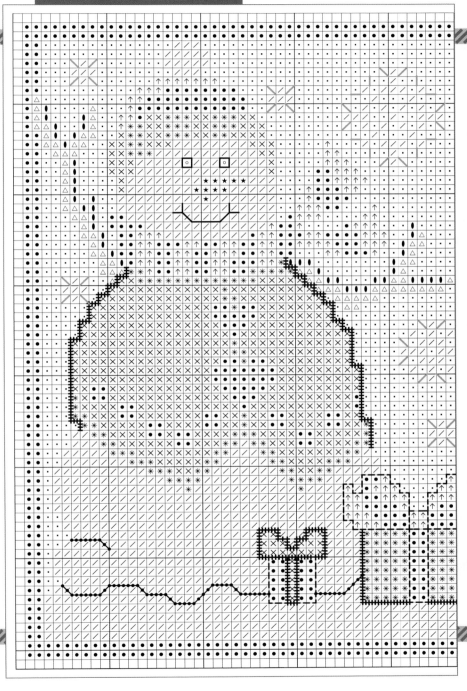

SNOWMAN (PART A)
92 × 72 threads

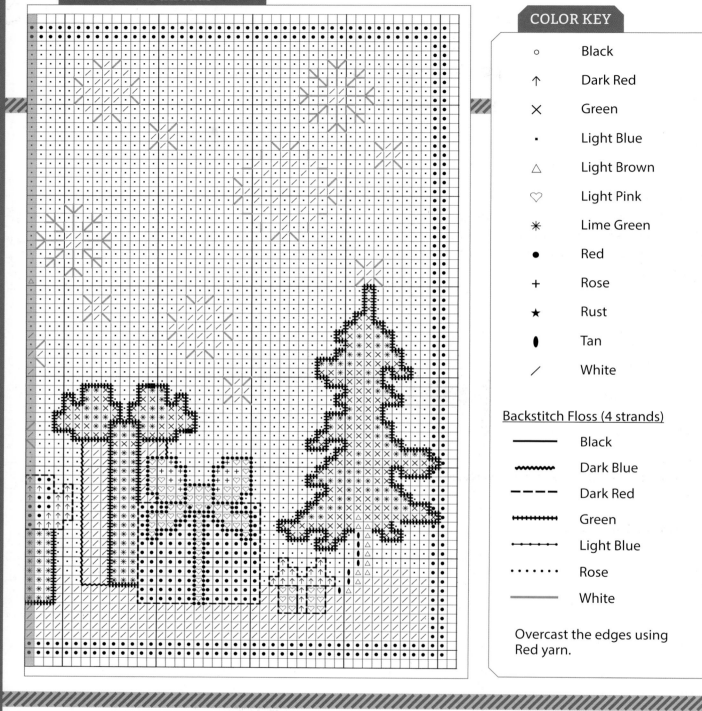

COLOR KEY

○	Black
↑	Dark Red
×	Green
·	Light Blue
△	Light Brown
♡	Light Pink
✳	Lime Green
●	Red
+	Rose
★	Rust
❙	Tan
╱	White

Backstitch Floss (4 strands)

———————	Black
∿∿∿∿∿∿	Dark Blue
— — — —	Dark Red
++++++++	Green
·—·—·—·	Light Blue
··········	Rose
———————	White

Overcast the edges using Red yarn.

Gray area indicates last row of previous section of design.